When is War Justified?

Andrew Goddard

Tutor in Ethics, Wycliffe Hall, Oxford

GROVE BOOKS LIMITED
RIDLEY HALL RD CAMBRIDGE CB3 9HU

Contents

Acknowledgments

My interest in issues of war and peace and the just war tradition began over ten years ago when attending lectures on the subject of justice, judgment and war by my doctoral supervisor, Professor Oliver O'Donovan. At that time I rather rashly wrote a paper for him on 'just war and pacifism' which dialogued critically with his lectures. I am most grateful to him not only for his careful comments on that but for assistance in many areas since then, especially in providing me with an early draft of his forthcoming *The Just War Revisited* (CUP, 2003) which draws together much of the material from his teaching that has shaped my own understanding of the tradition. Discussion with students I have taught at Wycliffe, especially James Maddern, have also helped to correct and clarify my thinking. Others who have particularly helped shape this booklet are the Grove Ethics Group (especially David Clough and Michael Beasley) and Nick Townsend who directs Sarum College's distance-learning Certificate in Politics and Theology. Despite their assistance, the views expressed in the booklet and its errors are, of course, my responsibility and not attributable to any of them.

The Cover Illustration is by Peter Ashton

First Impression January 2003
ISSN 1470-854X
ISBN 1 85174 520 3

Introduction

1

Living as we do in the midst of wars and rumours of wars it is vitally important that Christians think seriously about how to speak and act when nations take up arms against each other. When, if ever, is war justified?

The mainstream Christian reflection on war is represented by the Just War Tradition (JWT) and that is the focus here. It must, however, not be forgotten that there is a long-standing pacifist strand in Christian history which advocates a renunciation of all violence and participation in war on the part of Christians as a faithful witness to the way of Jesus Christ. This has revived in recent decades under the influence of such thinkers as John Howard Yoder and Stanley Hauerwas.[1] It has been complemented by the powerful analyses of writers such as Walter Wink and Jacques Ellul who uncover the destructive reality of violence, the phenomenon of the principalities and powers at work in our contemporary society, and the myth of redemptive violence which shapes so much Western, especially American, popular culture.[2] Although some of the insights from Christians who reject the JWT are drawn on, limited space prevents a proper account of the important Christian pacifist witness and the biblical material behind both the JWT and pacifist position.

The language of 'just war' is regularly misunderstood and misused by Christians, politicians and the media

The limited aim here is to introduce the JWT as a form of Christian moral reasoning and highlight its relevance at the start of the twenty-first century. Although the language of 'just war' dominates much debate and discussion, it is regularly misunderstood and misused by Christians, politicians and the media. The following chapters seek to explain the Christian rationale and pattern of thinking at the heart of the JWT. This underlying structure is often lost, and the practical and prophetic power of Christian reflection on war thereby muted when that rich tradition is reduced to a shopping list of test criteria against which any conflict is measured.

Chapter two offers an orientation to both the JWT as it has developed down the centuries and to the contemporary international context. The following three chapters discuss the two traditional parts of just war thinking—decisions about commencing war (*jus ad bellum*) in chapters three and four and decisions during war (*jus in bello*) in chapter five. The brief conclusion summarizes the main argument and places the detailed discussions of the central chapters within the bigger picture of the church's prophetic calling in the realm of international politics.

The power of Christian reflection on war is muted when this rich tradition is reduced to a shopping list of criteria

The Just War Tradition 2

Historical Development and Structure

The language of just war does not originate with Judaism or Christianity. Like the natural law tradition it finds its source in earlier classical thinking about warfare. The first significant (but far from systematic) Christian appropriation and transformation of that earlier thinking is found in the writings of Augustine. Building on Ambrose's thought, he developed a Christian defence of the use of lethal force by political authority basing it on love of neighbour. In contrast to some later just war thinkers, Augustine held that Christians had no right of self-defence against an aggressive neighbour. However, faced with a neighbour acting unjustly towards a third party, Christian love both *demanded* (coercive, even lethal) action to end the injustice out of love for the oppressed neighbour while *limiting* that action out of love for the neighbour who was an enemy.[3] This dual aspect of both authorizing and limiting the use of coercive force in war is at the heart of the Christian JWT.

Despite the tendency of some to refer to just war 'theory,' the language of 'tradition' is better. The JWT is not a fixed abstract theory but an evolving pattern of moral thought about justified warfare that has developed down the centuries. Following work by earlier medieval canon lawyers, Thomas Aquinas identified three requirements for a war to be just: sovereign authority to command war; just cause; and right intention.[4] He thereby innocently initiated a tendency to reduce just war thinking to criteria which later were understood as a checklist of tests to ascertain the justice of any potential or actual conflict. Such a method may have teaching value but risks losing the fundamental structure, theological rationale and prophetic dynamic of the tradition.

This dual aspect of both authorizing and limiting the use of coercive force in war is at the heart of the Christian JWT

The JWT is best understood as an attempt to conceptualize the political phenomenon of armed conflict in the light of the Christian gospel, the double command to love God and neighbour, and the divine provision of government in the face of human sin (Romans 13). It is primarily a proposal concerning the biblically mandated task of secular authority where it lacks recognized judicial processes through which it may act against wrongdoing. Although believing such action to be legitimate in some circumstances, it seeks to limit such action to responses to injustice and to structure any use of force by means of an analogy with the normal structure of acts of judgment against wrongdoing within the judicial system.[5]

The JWT seeks to structure any use of force by means of an analogy with the judicial system

This juridico-political structure, although evident in Aquinas, becomes particularly prominent during the sixteenth and seventeenth centuries. The works of both Roman Catholic (Francisco de Vitoria, 1485–1546 and Francisco Suarez, 1548–1617) and Protestant (Hugo Grotius, 1583–1645) theologians then revitalized medieval just war thinking in the face of such new challenges as the discovery of the New World and Christendom's fragmentation.[6] They provided the source and structure for the development of international law in relation to armed conflicts.

This ecumenical consensus developed little until the Second World War when the Anglican Bishop Bell and the Roman Catholic Fr John C Ford used just war moral reasoning to criticize saturation aerial bombing. Paul Ramsey then subsequently revived the tradition with a particular focus on the centrality of discrimination in the conduct of war.[7] The work of others who developed the JWT in the second half of the 20th century has, however, arguably disfigured that tradition in a manner that, though understandable in their context, removes some of its power in our different context. It is, therefore, important, before exploring the tradition in more detail and relating it to our situation, to trace the changing international context and some of the shifts in just war thinking in recent decades.

Just War Thinking During the Cold War Era

From the American decision to drop atomic bombs on Japan until the collapse of the Berlin Wall, many thinkers within the JWT focused on the nuclear threat in the context of the Cold War. International relations were marked by confrontation between two superpowers, each able to destroy the world several times over and to limit the UN's power and authority by use of their veto rights. There were, of course, numerous armed conflicts during this period, many involving the US and the USSR either directly or indirectly through support of surrogate forces in other countries. Of particular importance and with ramifications still today for US policy was the Vietnam conflict. All such regional conflicts were, however, conducted within limits set by recognized spheres of influence. All concerned were aware that destabilization risked escalation and the possible disaster of recourse to nuclear weapons (as with the 1962 Cuban missile crisis). Other conflicts were largely left to the warring parties and ignored by the wider international community (the 1981 Falklands War) although some provoked an international response and led to the end of conflict (the 1956 Suez Crisis).

Throughout these decades, a number of features stand out in the development of the JWT. The novelty of weapons of mass destruction was addressed in order to comment on and critique policies of weapons development, the theory of deterrence, and strategies of disarmament. In so doing, some Christians (such as John Stott) concluded that faithfulness to the JWT now required absolute opposition to any use of nuclear weaponry and became known as 'nuclear pacifists.' A similar move is evident in Roman Catholic thinking. Pope John XXIII's 1963 encyclical *Pacem in Terris*, declared, 'In this age which boasts of its atomic power, it no longer makes sense to maintain that war is a fit instrument with which to repair the violation of justice.'[8]

Partly as a result of this conclusion, partly from respect for the UN Charter,[9] the JWT began to be understood and widely popularized in terms of a condemnation of all first-use of military force. The tradition's determination to limit war here combined with a privileging of national sovereignty and a de-emphasizing of the pursuit of justice in order to restrict *jus ad bellum* to war in self-defence, a paradoxical conclusion for a tradition which looked back to Augustine as its originator.[10] It then became increasingly common to discern convergence between the traditionally opposed schools of just war and pacifism with writers claiming they share a common presumption against the use of force and in favour of peace understood as non-violence.[11] Whatever the merits of such a reconfiguration, these developments have in fact left the JWT weakened in our current post-Cold War context.

These developments have left the JWT weakened in our current post-Cold War context

The Changed Post-Cold War Climate

The moral questions raised by nuclear weapons must remain important in any contemporary Christian just war ethic. In particular, it must be asked whether those who themselves possess, maintain, develop (and in the past have used) such weapons have any morally cogent argument against non-nuclear states developing their own deterrent capability. Nevertheless, the international context of our thinking about war has changed, raising new issues and posing new challenges to the JWT. Four factors in particular must be noted.

First, the Soviet Union's demise leaves the United States as the sole global superpower. In the light of the imbalance of power that results from this change, the US could withdraw into isolationism or instead seek to use its position of strength for the common good of nations by acting as the 'world's policeman.' It could also be tempted to use its strength to defend its own interests and extend its power further. If it does not resist this temptation, we could witness unrestrained US imperialism and hegemony in international affairs given the lack of any nation or region with the political, economic or military strength to stand against it.

The JWT has always sought to recognize and respond to the concrete realities of power politics. This realignment within world politics must therefore lead to reassessment on the part of those who identify with this tradition. There is real danger in attempting to follow the line of thought advocated by the JWT without regard to the wider context of power within which all thinking about war must take place.

Second, the JWT has also always had to come to terms with how developing technology reshapes the nature of armed conflict. In addition to the continued reality of nuclear, chemical and biological weapons, two other factors must now be considered. In relation to weaponry, the development by wealthy powers of long-range missiles with elaborate targeting technology has brought a new form of distant warfare into play. This has led to an increasing imbalance in military and discriminatory power between those who have such weapons technology and those who lack it. In relation to our knowledge of war, the development of global communication networks (as first shown during the 1991 Gulf War) has also now resulted in an immediacy to at least some elements of war reporting. Populations far distant from the scene of conflict can become live spectators and instant (and so not necessarily reflective) commentators on the morality of the war.

Wars dominating our news agendas are not the only wars requiring us to think about justified war

The JWT must recognize these new developments and the new moral questions and temptations they raise while remembering that hi-tech wars watched from the comfort of our sitting room are still a small minority of the world's conflicts. Hundreds of thousands of Rwandans were killed in a few months with the most primitive forms of weaponry and relatively little media interest from the outside world. It is particularly important that Christians avoid the easy error of thinking that the only wars requiring us to think about justified war are those involving our own country or dominating our news agendas.

Third, as came home most powerfully on September 11ᵗʰ, non-state organizations now present a major threat to world peace and order. The JWT has recently sought to extricate itself from an inherent statism which seemed to rule out any justifiable use of force by non-governmental groups. It must now address those political authorities who seek to combat terrorist organizations. These organizations show no respect for the JWT and instead often understand war as total, holy war. Although some work has been done in this area, it is another important factor in our significantly changed context.[12]

> *JWT must now address those political authorities who seek to combat terrorist organizations*

Fourth, international arms trading and the quest by political authorities and non-governmental terrorist groups to secure weapons of mass destruction presents a challenge to the JWT. If that tradition seeks not only to guide those considering or already engaging in war but to guide Christian thinking about statecraft, justice and ordered peace in international affairs, then it cannot remain silent about this aspect of global affairs which fuels armed conflicts.[13]

The following chapters assess the value of traditional just war thinking in this changed context and in the light of recent conflicts. The great variety in the form of military conflicts is a further factor which must be considered and requires a realignment away from the overarching superpower conflict of the second half of the last century.[14]

Whatever the specifics of any conflict, the task of moral deliberation about war is helpfully distinguished into the two stages of prior to war (*ad bellum*) and during war (*in bello*). The following two chapters focus attention on thinking about recourse to war. They do so by asking and sketching answers to three questions—*why* war is to be waged (chapter three), and then *when* it is to be begun, and *who* is to wage it (chapter four). These are set within a moral theological framework controlled by a vision of the task of political authority—even in waging war—as the enacting of just judgment. This gives the traditionally listed criteria of *jus ad bellum* more substance and enables the tradition to speak to our contemporary context in a manner which rectifies some of its recent distortions. Chapter five turns its attention to the further moral questions which are added to these when war is being fought and examines the meaning and relevance of the principles of discrimination and proportion.

3 Justifying Going to War (i)

Why Wage War? Just Cause and Right Intention

The potential causes of war are numerous—expansionist goals, securing national or economic interests, removing unfriendly political leaders, racial or religious hatred, revenge, seeking personal or national glory. Faced with this plethora of causes for war, the juridical frame of reference in the JWT yields a two-fold justification for engaging in war. Looking *backwards*, it requires a *just cause* for war and understands this as the perpetration of a wrong by another party. Looking *forwards*, it seeks a *right intention* on the part of those fighting and limits wars to those intending to right such wrongs and establish a just peace.

What is a Just Cause?[15]

Within 'just cause,' the tradition has allowed a relatively wide range of 'wrongs' as potential legitimate reasons. Augustine illustrates 'wrong done' in terms of 'where punishment has to be meted out to a city or state because it has itself neglected to exact punishment for an offence committed by its citizens or subjects or to return what has been wrongfully taken away.' In contrast, much recent discussion of 'just cause' has restricted legitimate war to self-defence. However understandable and laudable as an attempt to limit war (especially given its modern destructiveness), this represents a significant revision, arguably a fundamental reversal, of the JWT's logic. In an era where wars of intervention are increasingly under consideration, it misleadingly suggests that the JWT prohibits all such actions.

Legitimate war can become tied to a self-interested defence of a nation's standing

Such a limited view of 'just cause' undermines the JWT's politically and juridically structured thinking. This is replaced with a self-protective and geographical rationale and so reduces 'right' to 'possession' and risks replacing 'justice' with 'self-interest.' Within the tradition, just war was understood as a political authority extending its task of opposing injustice beyond its established boundaries to where normal juridical processes are lacking or failing. Increasingly in modern times, however, legitimate war becomes tied to a self-interested defence of a nation's standing within the international community. This leaves a corrupt political authority secure from legitimate attack as long as it restricts its oppression, injustice and even genocide to within its own established and recognized borders. Every state becomes an island, secure from military action as long as it does not interfere with other 'islands.' As Kofi Annan (UN Secretary General) said in 1998, describing this understanding in terms of 'the old orthodoxy,'

> So long as the conflict rages within the borders of a single State, the old orthodoxy would require us to let it rage. We should leave it to 'burn itself out,' or perhaps to 'fester'...We should leave it even to escalate, regardless of human consequences, at least until the point when its effects begin to spill over into neighbouring States...[16]

That 'old orthodoxy' is not, however, the Christian JWT. This places at its heart the task of political authority to right wrongs, defend the poor and oppressed, and to punish evildoers.

Once this wider understanding of 'just cause' is understood three pressing issues are raised by the contemporary situation: the problem of popular moral judgment; the possibility of pre-emptive strikes; and the problem of selecting which injustices to tackle.

The Problem of Popular Moral Judgment
When war is not in response to a direct attack from an identifiable enemy the person in the street cannot easily judge whether a just cause exists. Governments often claim their concerns are based on 'intelligence' which cannot be made public and what is publicized is given the desired 'spin' by politicians and media coverage. The JWT was well aware of the information imbalance between rulers and ruled and overwhelmingly gave the benefit of doubt to the judgment of established authorities. It argued that they bear responsibility for any unjust war they knowingly initiate and that individual subjects should only oppose the judgment of their sovereign if they know for certain that no just cause exists for war.[17] Whether such a presumption about political leaders is still possible or desirable in our more egalitarian and democratic age (where we have learned the importance of a hermeneutic of suspicion in relation to power) is a serious challenge to this strand of the tradition.

The Possibility of Pre-emptive Strikes
A particular difficulty is raised with the growing call for a recognition of justified pre-emptive military action against a perceived threat and a strong

'first strike' policy in certain situations. This stands in stark contrast to the 'only in order to defend oneself against attack' understanding of just cause, appearing to justify 'getting our retaliation in first.' Set in the fuller understanding of the JWT the issues raised must be refocused by analogy with domestic juridical action against crime and driven by love for neighbour.

Parts of the JWT have been much more open to justifying such recourse to war than many realize. Thus Grotius refers to the Augustine passage cited above and writes,

> The grounds of war are as numerous as those of judicial actions. For where the power of law ceases, there war begins. Now there are methods in law to prevent intended injuries, as well as actions for those actually committed…St Augustine, in defining those to be just wars, which are made to avenge injuries has taken the word avenge in a general sense of removing and preventing, as well as punishing aggressions…A just cause then of war is an injury, which though not actually committed, threatens our persons or property with danger.[18]

In other words, just as the police are justified in detaining people believed to be preparing a serious crime rather than waiting for it to happen, so governments may be justified in taking action against other governments even before they carry out their wrongdoing.

Although the moral logic here is clear, the actual practice of pre-emptive action and preventive war is much more difficult to judge in particular cases. Grotius continues, in discussing Aquinas on self-defence, to stress that 'they are themselves much mistaken, and mislead others, who maintain that any degree of fear ought to be a ground for killing another, to prevent his *supposed* intention.'[19] Towards the end of his discussion Grotius's cautions are even clearer and pertinent to this contemporary question:

> Some writers have advanced a doctrine which can never be admitted, maintaining that the law of nations authorises one power to commence hostilities against another, whose increasing greatness awakens her alarms. As a matter of expediency such a measure may be adopted, but the principles of justice can never be advanced in its favour. The causes which entitle a war to the denomination of just are somewhat different from those of expediency alone. But to maintain that the bare probability of some remote, or future annoyance from a neighbouring state affords a just ground of hostile aggression, is a doctrine repugnant to every principle of equity. Such however is the condition of human life, that no full security can be enjoyed. The only protection against uncertain fears must

> be sought, not from violence, but from the divine providence, and defensive precaution. (*ibid* Book 2, 1.XVII)

In relation to military action against the terrorist threat or Iraq's alleged development of weapons of mass destruction, any appeal to this aspect of the JWT must be clear as to the moral wrong and alleged threatened 'injury.' It must take care that this is genuine and imminent and not simply based on supposition and playing on fear. It must also recall that a just cause—particularly one which leads to pre-emptive action—is never sufficient justification for recourse to war as other moral questions must be satisfactorily answered before war can be justified.

The Problem of Selectivity

Even a cursory comparison of the different international responses to recent situations of injustice in Bosnia, Kosovo, Rwanda and the Sudan, shows there is an important moral question of selectivity in which wrongs are responded to by war or the threat of military action.[20] There is rightly an outcry when a judicial system ignores certain serious wrongs or treats the same wrongs differently when committed by different groups. Those who speak up for just war must therefore be vigilant in drawing attention to possible just causes for military intervention. They should highlight evidence that something other than the pursuit of justice is guiding international policy and so reveal when appeals to 'just cause' are really hypocritical deceptions.

The church is particularly called to raise awareness of wrongs being perpetrated

The church, as an international communion committed to truth-telling, is particularly called to raise awareness of wrongs being perpetrated and requiring the attention of the international community. This is a double-edged sword. On the one hand, it could result in more conflicts as the agenda of combating international injustice would not be determined solely by whether a situation merits media coverage or serves the interests of one's own government and nation. On the other hand, the issue of selectivity may act as a restraint by raising such awkward questions as why the illicit development of nuclear weapons by India and Pakistan did not produce the same response from the global community as the alleged development of them now by Iraq.

Right Intention

Faced with selective response to injustice it is common to cast doubt on the motives of political leaders. This usually takes such form as 'the real reason why we are fighting this war is…,' with some aspect of domestic politics or alleged economic benefit then cited. Motives in war are clearly not exempt from moral scrutiny. Augustine famously commented that the real evil in war was not the death of people who would soon die anyway but rather 'love of violence, revengeful cruelty, fierce and implacable enmity, wild resistance and the lust of power.'[21] However, others' motivations (particularly those of that peculiar moral agent 'political authority') are very difficult to discern (especially in a pre-emptive strike). When questioning of motives is smuggled into discussion of 'right intention' an error has occurred due to a failure to distinguish intention from motive.[22]

The language of 'intention' seeks to clarify an action's goal and purpose from its structure. The language of 'motive' goes behind this to the agent's desires and larger schemes. So, I may regularly visit an aging sick relative. Such action intends to provide them with the care and company they need and would otherwise lack. My motive, however, may be to ensure that I, rather than my brother, benefit in the will. Similarly, the intention in recourse to war may be removal of an invading and oppressive power from occupation of an oil-rich neighbour. My motivation may, however, be to secure continued supply of cheap oil. Such ulterior motives could be revealed at some future stage as a result of my actions (for example, ceasing to oppose the invading force once assured that cheap oil is not threatened, or stopping visits once my relative is too ill to alter her will). Until that happens, however, an action which has a good end in view cannot be judged illegitimate solely on the basis of a suspicion that the good end is not the ultimate goal that motivates a particular agent.

Christians must examine their own motives and challenge others—including political leaders—to do likewise. The focus of concern, however, cannot be this hidden subjective realm but the scrutiny of public statements as to intent and the analysis of the actions in order to judge whether they truly serve that stated intention.[23]

The right intention required in entering (and prosecuting) war is, simply, to right the wrong which provided the justificatory cause for resort to force. This means intending such ends as the punishment of those who have done wrong, rectifying their evil acts, and the liberation of the oppressed. Augustine summed this up in the paradox of going to war intending peace.

Peace should be the object of your desire; war should be waged only as a necessity, and waged only that God may by it deliver men from the necessity and preserve them in peace...war is waged in order that peace may be obtained...[24]

Justifying Going to War (ii) 4

When Wage War? Last Resort and Likely Outcome

In speaking of war being waged 'only as a necessity,' Augustine highlights that, because it is such a great physical evil, war must never be entered lightly or precipitously. The existence of an injustice is never in itself sufficient for justifying resort to war. In seeking justice outside its normal jurisdiction, political authority has many alternative weapons such as diplomatic protest, negotiation and concerted international sanctions before recourse to war.[25]

This concern of the JWT is summed up in terms of war as a *last resort*. The terminology is again open to misunderstanding on the grounds that another form of non-military sanction or period of negotiations is always available. In fact, within the broader context of enacting just judgment, 'last resort' proves once again a double-edged sword. On the one hand, it pressurizes authorities to find peaceful means of conflict resolution and warns against unnecessary short-term negotiation deadlines or resorting to war whenever domestic public opinion has been softened up sufficiently to support military action. On the other hand, 'last resort' can set a timetable after which either war must be engaged or else the injustice counted as among the many which must await resolution by divine providence or God's final judgment. So, if we must do all we legitimately can to remove some occupying force and the onset of winter makes a military campaign to do so impossible unless that campaign begins by a certain time, then that time becomes the time of legitimate 'last resort' ('now or never').

Within the broader context of enacting just judgment, 'last resort' proves a double-edged sword

The other factor in considering whether this is a time for war is its *likely outcome*. Whether expressed in terms of 'reasonable prospect of success' or the more utilitarian 'resulting in more good than evil,' this is again liable to misunderstanding. Detached from the politico-juridical moral framework of the JWT, it is easily subsumed within the widespread consequentialist moral world-view. There the rightness or wrongness of actions is determined solely by the consequences; moral decision-making involves calculating such consequences. At its worst this leads to arguments such as 'everyone can see that regime change in Iraq will result in a better situation for Iraq, the region, and the world and therefore this criterion of a just war is met.'

Within the paradigm of war as an act of judgment, thinking about the outcome is, like last resort, an element of the need for 'proportionate response.' It reminds us that just as other less destructive means must be used rather than war if they can secure our desired end of righting wrong, so, if a justly waged war is unable to secure that desired end and establish an ordered peace then it must not even be started.

The JWT often appealed to medical analogies and this may illuminate deliberation about when to go to war. War is like a major operation on the human body. In considering whether now is the time to operate, the surgeon must not only know what is wrong and seek to put it right. She is also morally obliged to ask whether any other less risky procedure is currently available and likely to succeed (last resort) and to weigh the probability of the proposed surgery accomplishing the desired end (reasonable prospect). If she knows some other option is likely to succeed and will put her patient at less risk she is culpable if she does not use that option (although a time may also come when unless she now attempts the riskier option the patient will die). Likewise if she knows that the major operation will not achieve what is required or that it will do so only at disproportionate risk or cost to the patient's life or welfare then she must refrain from action.

Moving back from this analogy to the reality of war, the final question is 'who, then, is the doctor?'

Who Wages War?—Legitimate Authority

> In order for a war to be just, three things are necessary. First, the authority of the sovereign by whose command the war is to be waged. For it is not the business of a private individual to declare war...[26]

Aquinas here succinctly sums up the JWT's emphatic primary restriction on who may legitimately wage war. He confirms that, to understand it properly, the JWT must be located within a broader theological account of political authority whose biblical focus is Romans 13. What is significant today in relation to that developing tradition is the tendency (already noted) to limit 'just cause' to self-defence. This means that effectively the only legitimate authority to wage war is a state which comes under attack. But if legitimate authority is understood to reside solely with the political authority whose people come under attack (and usually, by extension, other political authorities whom it may enlist in its cause as Kuwait did following Iraq's invasion), then the JWT's politically and juridically structured thinking has been forgotten. As we have seen, such a political philosophy neglects those neighbours who lack the status of recognized states. To counter it, it is necessary to recall that the JWT never understood 'legitimate authority' to mean that the war-making power must already be acknowledged as the legitimate and recognized political authority of those on whose behalf it went to war. As the passage from Aquinas makes clear, the fundamental concern of the tradition was the contrast of 'the authority of the sovereign' with 'a private individual.'

Does this therefore mean that any political authority has a right to go to war? Even where their own people are not being wronged? Even if war involves 'interference' within the established boundaries of a sovereign state? Is this not liable to become, in the current context, a legitimation of American imperialism? The dangers in such an understanding are clear. Kofi Annan asks, 'Can we really afford to let each State be the judge of its own right, or duty, to intervene in another State's internal conflict? If we do, will we not be forced to legitimize Hitler's championship of the Sudeten Germans, or Soviet intervention in Afghanistan?'[27]

Neither NATO nor the EU can claim to be a genuine supra-national political authority

While there are real dangers here, two features of the tradition provide assistance. *First*, particularly during the multi-layered structures of political authority found within feudal medieval Christendom, much debate occurred concerning where (from the local knight to the Emperor) political authority to initiate war should be located. Reflecting the desire to limit and control war, the tendency was to place authority at as high a level as possible within the political hierarchy and so in very few hands. The difficulty with drawing on this today is that, although undergoing change, the political authority to command within most societies still reaches its zenith with sovereign nation-states. Within the Western world, for example, neither NATO nor the EU can claim to be a genuine supra-national political authority. Neither institution has both the recognized right to enact judgment within its own borders and the power to enforce such judgments in a way which would make it conform to the JWT's conception of a legitimate political authority.

Internationally, the United Nations is the most obvious body to overcome this limitation. It too, however, is not a recognized governing power whose writ runs within a political community. In relation to its ability to use coercive force against agents of injustice, it is so reliant on the initiative and the commitment of member sovereign states (particularly its most powerful) that one is reminded of Stalin's comment, 'The Pope! How many divisions has *he* got?' Paul Ramsey's critique over 40 years ago sadly still applies today when thinking about the need for a legitimate political authority which can act in more than self-defence, 'Protestants often seem to suppose that the way to "strengthen the UN" is to speak as if it already had the strength and therefore no nation the right of war.'[28] Unless and until regional or global structures of political authority change so these structures (rather than nation states) are both recognized and empowered to act juridically and coercively within their own boundaries, legitimate authority to wage just war must—from the outlook of the JWT—be held to reside with existing sovereign political authorities.

Legitimate authority to wage just war must be held to reside with existing sovereign political authorities

Secondly, this need not, however, result in *carte blanche* acceptance of any and every military intervention by a powerful sovereign state. The whole juridical paradigm—requiring those who enter war to do so viewing themselves as acting in judgment on behalf of those whose right they seek to defend—adds a number of caveats. Viewed in this manner it would appear preferable that there should be some connection between those who act and those on whose behalf they use force. While they would strictly meet the requirement of having legitimate authority, non-defensive interventions in another state by an outside authority without request for military support (preferably from an alternative political authority in waiting) and where there are no historic or regional links to the area of conflict will be highly problematic.

Furthermore, where a sovereign power acts against another which is not directly attacking it (especially when it claims authority to judge another sovereign power for actions within its own jurisdiction or to act to prevent a possible future injustice) such decisions have greater moral weight if that power does not act alone. Rather than appearing to advance its own interests, it should evidently represent the judgment of the wider international community. Such a situation applied in relation to the 1991 Gulf War where there was both an international coalition and a UN resolution authorizing the use of force. There may, however, be a developing tendency in certain places to bypass the UN and even to ignore the consensus of international opinion.

In summary, any existing political authority could claim the tradition authorizes it to initiate war. However, unwillingness to put the case for an offensive war to the UN raises real doubts as to whether such conflicts are conforming to the requirement that war should be limited and seek to enact just judgment. Although the rhetoric of 'just war' may still be being used, the terminology is then in danger of becoming an ideological fig-leaf for a morally denuded foreign policy.

Before turning to what is justified during war, one final contemporary issue is raised under the question of legitimate authority. The JWT clearly cannot justify acts of indiscriminate, international terrorist networks (such as Al Qaeda) which are totally divorced from the working of political institutions committed to the enacting of just judgment. The more difficult question is how it guides government responses to such acts. A strong case can be made that they are best viewed as criminal offences because the punishment of them is more easily incorporated within existing structures of judicial process. On such a view, anti-terrorist action will be more effectively prosecuted by normal legal means on a global scale than by unilateral or even multilateral military action. This will probably require innovations in the structures and authority of international courts which, given US attitudes to the new International Criminal Court, may prove unwelcome in some powerful countries. However, as the lethal power in the hands of terrorists becomes equivalent to that in the hands of legitimate sovereign states, this analysis becomes less plausible and recourse to war more justifiable.

'Just war' terminology is then in danger of becoming an ideological fig-leaf for a denuded foreign policy

Much current thinking here clearly still lacks conceptual clarity. This is sadly encouraged by such phrases as 'war against terrorism' where both 'war' and 'terrorism' are sweeping and ill-defined terms which fail to focus the moral structure of the actions being proposed and undertaken. As a result, there is real danger that such a 'war' will cease to be subject to the constraints of just judgment in both its end and means. It is liable then to become an ideological, religious and total war with normal juridical safeguards in both domestic and international law being overthrown in the face of 'emergency situations.'

5 Justifying the Conduct of War

'All's fair in love and war' leads to the conclusion that whatever careful moral deliberation is possible or required in the cold reasoned decision-making about going to war, once that decision is made moral concerns are no longer necessary, as the end now justifies the means.

From this perspective, all means judged necessary to win the war are legitimate. The JWT, in contrast, has insisted that the concept of war as a form of judgment must also control war's prosecution. This means that those issues discussed in the last two chapters remain morally relevant once war has commenced. When, for example, war fought justly can no longer achieve a just peace or alternative means are open to secure this end then the continued justifiability of war must be questioned. It also follows that military actions must themselves be subject to judgment. In particular they must be shown to be *discriminating* (as judgment seeks to punish the guilty and rescue the innocent) and *proportionate* (as in judgment, punishment must fit the crime).

Discrimination—Legitimate and Illegitimate Targets

'It is in no way lawful to slay the innocent' (Aquinas). 'The deliberate slaughter of the innocent is never lawful in itself' (Vitoria). Last century, these clear statements from the tradition were strongly reaffirmed by Paul Ramsey throughout his writing. There he spelled out what he understood discrimination to mean in relation to war:

> In determining justifiable and unjustifiable warfare, the work of love will be to return ever again to the prohibition of the direct killing of any person not directly or closely co-operating in the force that should be repelled.[29]

Looking back on war in the last century, two apparently opposing trends appear. On the one hand, we find careful implementation of this fundamental moral truth within international humanitarian law, the laws of war and some developments in weapons technology. On the other hand, there is a much more discouraging concrete reality:

> In the First World War, roughly 90% of those killed were soldiers, and only 10% civilians. In the Second World War, even if we count all the victims of Nazi death camps as war casualties, civilians made up only half, or just over half, of all those killed. But in many of today's conflicts, civilians have become the main targets of violence. It is now conventional to put the proportion of civilian casualties somewhere in the region of 75%.[30]

Faced with this disparity it is important to clarify the language of discrimination and note contemporary challenges to it. Ramsey's statement clarifies what the tradition means to outlaw: intending the direct killing of any person who is not directly or closely co-operating in the force one is opposing. War is not waged against a whole society, all of whose members are to be judged equally guilty enemies. It is rather action against an injustice and against all those materially involved in that wrongdoing.

A number of brief clarifications must be made here. *First*, the death of civilians does not necessarily prove violation of this prohibition. In contrast to consequentialist moral thinking, the outcome of the act alone does not determine whether that act was right or wrong. *Secondly*, the tradition has clarified its prohibition in terms of the principle of 'double effect.' An action we can foresee will entail the death of innocent people may, nevertheless, be legitimate in war under certain circumstances just as within domestic criminal justice we foresee that innocent people (such as the family and friends of the criminal) will suffer as a result of punishing guilty criminals. The euphemism 'collateral damage' is unpleasant and often abused but the JWT has always recognized that in war,

Within domestic criminal justice we foresee that innocent people will suffer as a result of punishing guilty criminals

even while strictly aiming at legitimate targets, innocent bystanders will often suffer from the (second, double or side) effect of military action. This reality may render such action illegitimate (for example, if the secondary and unintended innocent suffering is excessive and disproportionate) but it need not always and necessarily do so.

These clarifications of the meaning of 'discrimination' are important faced with such often unhelpful short-hand summaries as 'noncombatant immunity' or 'no attacks on civilians.' It is clear that, even with these qualifications, much war today disregards this central plank of just war thinking. The primary task of those in the JWT is therefore to insist that discrimination must shape the conduct of war.[31] Even when this happens, however, there are novel challenges to be faced today. Four, in particular, merit brief discussion.

First, whereas in much Western history (and still today in many areas of conflict) a distinction can be relatively easily drawn between legitimate and illegitimate targets for direct attack, this becomes more complex in integrated, technological societies. The difficulty relates to both people and material infrastructure. During the war in Kosovo, for example, NATO forces decided certain media outlets were legitimate targets on the grounds they were tools of state propaganda spreading deception and seeking to increase commitment to the war. Given the growing importance and power of communication technologies in modern war, such an argument has more plausibility than in the past. It is, however, hard to believe the British government would ever accept the BBC could be a legitimate target for our enemies. Similarly, attacks on power supplies because they are essential to military networks and so a legitimate target for direct attack cannot simply be accepted. It must be recognized that most of those who work there are not guilty of material co-operation in war but simply serving civil society. Disabling such installations also harms many innocent people reliant on them for basic needs. In a world where wider civil society and state institutions share dependence on an interconnected network of technologies and more and more of the population live in cities close to centres of political and military power, greater thought needs to be given as to what 'discrimination in attack' means in practice.

> *A distinction between legitimate and illegitimate targets becomes more complex in integrated, technological societies*

Secondly, partly due to these changes and a commitment to discrimination, much modern weapons technology seeks to be 'smart' through using precision guided munitions and target acquisition systems.[32] The use of such systems means that proper scrutiny must be given to the accuracy of information used in the deployment of such weapons. The apparently accidental NATO attack on the Chinese Embassy in Belgrade due to the use of an out-of-date map vividly illustrates that responsibilities here are not always taken seriously. An appeal to an intention to discriminate in war lacks credibility if little or no care is taken to discover whether or not the target claimed to be legitimate is actually the target one claims it to be.[33] It is also important to realize that, even with modern technology, the use of aerial bombing and guided missiles is not as accurate as many think in effecting discrimination.

Even official Pentagon figures claimed that only 75% of the munitions dropped by Navy and Marine Corps aircraft in Afghanistan destroyed or disabled the intended target (a distinct improvement on the Gulf and Kosovo campaigns where roughly half were effective).[34]

Thirdly, discrimination is (unsurprisingly) more difficult to achieve when distant from enemy forces, particularly if legitimate and illegitimate targets are in close proximity. While building discriminatory capabilities into missiles is welcome, the over-reliance on such forms of long-distance warfare must be questioned. There is clearly a concern on the part of technologically rich, democratic regimes that any conflict must minimize the domestic 'body bag' count. Even more dubious there is often a concern to protect expensive, hi-tech military equipment from damage. The official US evaluation of the Gulf air campaign of 1991 notes that commanders favoured, 'strike tactics that maximized aircraft and pilot survivability rather than weapon system effectiveness' and that 'the use of medium- to high-altitude munition delivery tactics…both reduced the accuracy of guided and unguided munitions and hindered target identification and acquisition.'[35] Simply put this comes close to saying that concern for protection of their own combat forces and material resources was held so important that protecting noncombatants from indiscriminate or disproportionate attack played little role in US tactics.

> *Over-reliance on such forms of long-distance warfare must be questioned*

Fourthly, there is a real danger the world's most powerful military nations believe justice can only be sought in war if the human cost to them is negligible or nonexistent. Any commitment to careful discrimination between combatants and noncombatants is then weakened or lost when such discrimination requires a more realistic assessment of the risks involved for domestic military personnel. This undermines appeals to the JWT, creating a distorted perception of the reality of war and the costliness of any genuine desire to enact justice in our fallen world.[36] If policy is shaped not by justice for the oppressed but gaining one's desired ends at as little personal cost as possible, this will also lead to an unwillingness to act against injustices which could perhaps be brought to an end but only at the cost of suffering some, perhaps not insignificant, losses (as in Rwanda and Bosnia).

Christians committed to the JWT as a pattern of moral reasoning faithful to God's revelation in the person and work of Jesus Christ must make clear the necessary pain and cost to be suffered if one is committed to enacting just judgment in a fallen world. This must be faced and endured rather than avoided and denied by those who, in the name of justice, have the power to impose their will on those who are relatively powerless.

Proportion—Means and Ends

'Don't use a sledgehammer to crack a nut.' This is the heart of the JWT's understanding of proportion. It is emphatically not an authorization for a tit-for-tat ratcheting up the levels of destructive force. It does not mean that if the enemy has recourse to nuclear weapons then these become a legitimate proportionate response. To speak of proportion during war is to scrutinize which means are best fitted to achieve the desired end. Within the JWT this means that action must be measured by the nature of the injustice being opposed (some crimes merit greater force than others) and the goals set in countering that injustice by coercive force.

This line of thought might, once again, work in one of two ways. It could judge any particular action as disproportionate because it does not do enough to achieve its end. More commonly an action will be disproportionate because it does too much ('overkill') or fails to serve the end being sought (for example if it is simply a demonstration of power *pour encourager les autres*).

Decisions about proportion were discussed in the last chapter in relation to when to go to war. During war, they are generally much more flexible in nature than decisions about discrimination and thus more difficult to discuss in the abstract. Three contemporary concerns must, however, be noted.

First, there is currently a great global imbalance in military power. This creates a two-fold challenge. On the part of those with relatively little power there is the strong temptation, faced with such disproportion, to resort to indiscriminate means (of which terrorist attacks are the most extreme). These can appear the most likely way to achieve political ends that are being opposed by those with power but their essentially indiscriminate nature makes them wholly illegitimate from the perspective of the Christian JWT. On the part of those with great power there is the danger (especially given the desire for limiting home casualties) of excessive levels of force being used without reference to the political ends being sought. The levels of explosives dropped on Kosovo (a region about the size of Wales) and Afghanistan perhaps illustrate this.

Sadly neither modern media-dominated democracies nor non-democratic regimes are conducive to careful deliberation

Secondly, the relative failure in the case of Afghanistan to achieve the desired political ends suggests the military means used were not fully suited to those ends. As the threats to a just and peaceful world order are changing, the requirement for proportionate response may well require changes in standard military strategies, forms of weapons systems and military training in order that war may be conducted justly and in a manner proportionate to the end in view.

Thirdly, the need to mobilize and maintain popular support for military action often results in propaganda that increasingly demonizes one's enemies. This is true whether it is the US as 'the Great Satan' or an 'axis of evil.' This in turn can lead to the acceptance of disproportionate means of war due to an exaggerated and distorted perception of the wrong which war is seeking to right. Some unjust acts require much more force than others to oppose and rectify them. There is, however, the need for sober and careful assessment of what would be a disproportionate response. Sadly neither modern media-dominated democracies nor non-democratic regimes are conducive to such careful deliberation.

Conclusion 6

This booklet has not attempted to defend the JWT against its many critics.

It has sought instead to explain its structure and rationale and highlight the agenda and questions it raises in the current international context as people ask whether war is justified. In doing so it has criticized certain popular (mis)understandings and recent reformulations of the mainstream tradition. It has presented the JWT as a pattern of conceptualizing the political task in international affairs, including the use of military force, in terms of exercising judgment beyond the normal juridical procedures.

Stepping back from the detailed decision-making and specific focused questions and 'criteria,' the value of the JWT as a whole is that it encourages and enables the Christian church to be practical and constructive but also to have a distinctive and prophetic task in relation to political power. When properly appropriated, the JWT is not simply an uncritical pro-establishment stance towards political authority. It stands in condemnation of much standard thinking and practice about the nature of war and international politics even though this sometimes claims to represent just war thinking. It presents a challenge to discern and speak the truth about injustice and the forms in which obeying the command to love our neighbour might shape the task of political authority as it seeks justice in international politics.

Awaiting the fullness of God's kingdom of justice and peace, the JWT acknowledges that political authority is authorized to use limited levels of coercive force in order to restrain evil and liberate the oppressed. Political authority may do this not only inside its borders by use of the police and judicial processes but even outside its borders. But at its best the JWT also knows that the kingdoms of this fallen world are often eager to assert themselves and increase their power. Political powers do not easily admit they are passing away and will be destroyed by the reign of God (1 Cor 15.24). They often see themselves as able to redeem and vanquish evil. The truth is that they can never, in this present evil age of which they are part, bring in the coming kingdom of justice and peace. That kingdom is the reign

The JWT is not simply an uncritical pro-establishment stance towards political authority

of the crucified and risen Messiah, the kingdom of which Jesus said, 'My kingdom is not of this world...if it were my servants would fight to prevent my arrest by the Jews' (Jn 18.36). Praying for the coming of that kingdom and bearing witness to it in both word and deed is the supreme calling and task of the church, in times of war and in times of relative peace.

Notes

1   The best known works of Yoder are *The Original Revolution: Essays on Christian Pacifism* (Herald Press, 1971), *Nevertheless: Varieties of Religious Pacifism* (Herald Press, 1992, revised edn) and *The Politics of Jesus* (Paternoster, 1994, 2nd edn). On his work see now Craig A Carter, *The Politics of the Cross: The Theology and Social Ethics of John Howard Yoder* (Brazos Press, 2001). Hauerwas' main study is *The Peaceable Kingdom* (SCM Press, 1984) and essays in *Against the Nations* (Notre Dame, 1992) and *Dispatches From the Front* (Duke UP, 1994). A biblical critique of violence in defence of justice is found in Richard B Hays, *The Moral Vision of the New Testament* (T & T Clark, 1996) ch 14.

2   Jacques Ellul, *Violence* (SCM, 1970) and Walter Wink's 'powers' trilogy, especially *Engaging the Powers* (Fortress, 1992). A response to current situation influenced from this perspective is Lee Griffith, *War on Terrorism and the Terror of God* (Eerdmans, 2002).

3   The key texts from Augustine can be found in O'Donovan and O'Donovan, *From Irenaeus to Grotius: A Sourcebook in Christian Political Thought* (Eerdmans, 1999) and in Gill, *A Textbook of Christian Ethics* (T & T Clark, 1995) pp 266–76. This reading of Augustine owes much to Paul Ramsey, *War and the Christian Conscience* (Duke UP, 1961).

4   The key text here is the *Summa Theologiae II/II*, q40.

5   This characterization of just war thinking owes much to the work of O'Donovan, first sketched in the Grove booklet, *In Pursuit of a Christian View of War*.

6   This analogical pattern of thinking is, of course, evident in Aquinas *eg* 'Just as it is lawful for them [those in authority] to have recourse to the sword in defending that commonweal against internal disturbances, when they punish evildoers, according to the words of the Apostle (Rom 13.4)…so, too, it is their business to have recourse to the sword of war in defending the commonweal against external enemies.' Vitoria argues that 'a prince when at war has by right of war the same authority over the enemy as if he were their lawful judge and prince.'

7   In addition to *War and the Christian Conscience*, Paul's Ramsey's main works are the essays collected in *The Just War* (UPA, 1968) and *Speak Up for Just War or Pacifism* (Penn State UP, 1988) with Stanley Hauerwas. Ramsey's work remains indispensable for Christians seeking to draw on the JWT although his concern with pressing contemporary issues in American foreign policy limits the direct relevance of some of his work today.

8   *Pacem in Terris*, para 127.

9   The UN Charter prohibits member states from 'the threat or use of force against the territorial integrity or political independence of any state' (Article 2) while insisting that 'nothing in the present Charter shall impair the inherent right of individual or collective self-defence if an armed attack occurs against a Member of the United Nations' (Article 51).

10   Influenced by the work of Michael Walzer (*Just and Unjust Wars*), Richard Norman comments, '"Just war" thinking has increasingly, and especially in its secular versions, come to focus on one specific justification for war…The only justification for going to war is…as *defence against aggression*…' (*Ethics, Killing and War*, CUP, 1995, pp 119–120).

11   For rebuttal of this view see Joseph E Capizzi, 'On Behalf of the Neighbor: A Rejection of the Complementarity of Just-War Theory and Pacifism' *Studies in Christian Ethics* 14.2, pp 87–108.

12   Ramsey has an essay in *The Just War* on 'counter-insurgency' war (pp 427–64) and, more recently, see James Turner Johnson, 'In Response to Terror,' *First Things*, 90 (Feb 1999) pp 11–13.

13   Robin Gill addresses this in 'The arms trade and Christian ethics' in his *Cambridge Companion to Christian Ethics* (CUP, 2001) pp 183–94.

14   Although not exhaustive, the following list sketches the major different scenarios which it seems the JWT now needs to be capable of addressing if it is to remain of value in the new millennium: (a) Border disputes between sovereign states (*eg* India and Pakistan over Kashmir); (b) International alliances against an alleged 'rogue state' (*eg* War in Afghanistan, Gulf War on behalf of Kuwait against Iraq); (c) Intervention where political authority is lacking and society is descending into anarchy (*eg* Rwanda, Somalia, former Yugoslavia); (d) Intervention where political authority is acting unjustly within its own borders (*eg* Serbia in Kosovo, South Africa under apartheid);

(e) Intervention in the face of humanitarian crises (*eg* Iraqi Kurds post Gulf war, Kosovo); (f) Response to disputed declarations of independence by new political authorities (*eg* Bosnia and former Yugoslavia, Chechnya and other former Soviet republics); (g) Response to attacks from non-governmental terrorist organizations (*eg* Al-Qaeda and US war against terrorism)

15   For a recent excellent discussion discovered too late to incorporate into this argument see James Turner Johnson's 'Just Cause Revisited' on the web at www.eppc.org

16   Kofi Annan, *The Question of Intervention* (UN Dept of Public Information, 1999) pp 5–6.

17   Aquinas writes that 'the person by whose authority a thing is done really does the thing,' while Vitoria states 'other lesser folk who have no place or audience in the prince's council or in the public council are under no obligation to examine the causes of war, but may serve in it in reliance on their betters…Nevertheless the proofs and tokens of the injustice of the war may be such that ignorance would be no excuse even to subjects of this sort who serve in it.'

18   Hugo Grotius, *The Rights of War and Peace*, Bk 2, 1.II. This important text is now available on the web at http://www.constitution.org/gro/djbp.htm

19   *ibid*, Bk 2, 1.V.

20   For a damning critique of UK policy in Bosnia see Brendan Simms, *Unfinest Hour* (Penguin, 2002). In Rwanda, Kofi Annan has acknowledged that the commander of the UN mission there said 'that 5,000 peacekeepers could have saved 500,000 lives' (*op cit*, p 12). The reality of such unwillingness to act is powerfully demonstrated in the moving personal stories in Elizabeth Neuffer, *The Key to My Neighbour's House* (Bloomsbury, 2002).

21   Augustine, *Contra Faustus* in Gill, *A Textbook of Christian Ethics* (T & T Clark, 1995) p 273.

22   Norman, *op cit*, p 118 in explaining right intention in relation to *jus ad bellum* criteria signals the distinction by adding to his account of right intention, 'not with ulterior motives.'

23   This focus on right intention related to just cause highlights the importance of clear (although not inflexible) war aims. This is always a crucial element in moral discussion of war, a lesson evident in the Gulf War with debates over whether the aim was to expel Iraq from Kuwait or also to protect Iraqi Kurds or even occupy Baghdad.

24   Augustine, *Letter 189 to Boniface* in O'Donovan and O'Donovan, *op cit*, p 135. Luther speaks of being 'forced into peace' and of a just war as 'the punishment of evildoers and the maintenance of peace.'

25   As international action against another regime moves up this scale of coercion, the actions increasingly take on the character of acts of war and the moral constraints developed within the JWT become more and more applicable. For example, it is now clear that the ongoing use of economic sanctions against Iraq have significantly harmed Iraqi society in a manner which is not dissimilar to traditional acts of war and that the damage has been much more indiscriminate than much warfare.

26   Aquinas *Summa II/II*, q40 a1 *sed contra*.

27   Annan, *op cit*, p 10.

28   Paul Ramsey, *War and Christian Conscience*, p 85.

29   *Ibid*, p 190.

30   Annan, *op cit*, p 5.

31   For other examples of how widespread is disregard for this and other elements of just war thinking as enshrined in international law see www.crimesofwar.org

32   Although these 'smart' systems may involve technology such as radar and laser guidance, the website www.globalsecurity.org helpfully informs us that 'Target Acquisition (TA) systems include the human eye which is the most commonly employed TA system'!

33   The bombing of a wedding party by US aircraft in Afghanistan is yet another example of the importance of this principle.

34   It was widely reported that a secret Ministry of Defence report into RAF missiles fired in Kosovo discovered only 40% were accurate. It must be remembered that even those nations with advanced technology continue to use less sophisticated and accurate weaponry which is likely to be much more indiscriminate (for example the UK dropped over 200 unguided 1,000lb bombs on Kosovo as well as over 500 cluster bombs which explode before impact and drop numerous bomb-lets over a large area).

35   Summary of report on http://www.fas.org/man/gao/nsiad97134/summary.htm.

36   The enormous death toll from the World Trade Centre stands in sharp contrast with the fact that only 148 US military were killed in action in the Gulf War (compared with at least 100,000 Iraqi soldiers). This experience of 'low-cost' war is bound to have an important effect on a nation.

All the links listed here are live on the Grove web site which also contains further information and resources http://www.grovebooks.co.uk